The National Archives

THE GUNPOWDER PLOT

UNCLASSIFIED

Secrets of the Gunpowder Plot Revealed

NICK HUNTER

A & C BLACK
AN IMPRINT OF BLOOMSBURY
LONDON NEW DELHI NEW YORK SYDNEY

Published 2014 by A & C Black,
an imprint of Bloomsbury Publishing Plc,
50 Bedford Square
London, WC1B 3DP

www.bloomsbury.com

Bloomsbury is a registered trademark of Bloomsbury Publishing Plc

Design by Nick Avery Design

ISBN: 978-1-4729-0856-8

A CIP catalogue for this book is available from the British Library.

Printed in China by Leo Paper Products, Heshan, Guangdong

1 3 5 7 9 10 8 6 4 2

CONTENTS

DISCOVERED!

Tuesday 5 November 1605 was going to be a day to remember. England's Houses of Parliament in London would be packed with the country's most powerful nobles gathered for the opening of Parliament by King James I. London was just recovering from a terrible outbreak of plague and the ceremony would be a glorious day for king and country.

▲ *The plot was big news across Europe. This Dutch print shows the moment the Gunpowder Plot was discovered.*

But not everyone wished the King well. Government forces were on high alert in case any enemies of the King tried to disrupt this great state occasion. On the night of 4 November, the King himself ordered a search of Parliament. They had discovered a clear warning that England's ruler was in mortal danger.

In a cellar beneath the House of Lords, the search party made one of the most sensational discoveries in history. They found enough gunpowder to destroy Parliament and everyone in it. After a struggle, they seized a man who gave his name as 'John Johnson'.

The Gunpowder Plot revealed

The search had uncovered a daring plot to blow up Parliament and kill the King. Who were the plotters, what did they want, and how close did they come to changing the course of history? This book looks at incredible documents more than 400 years old to uncover the secrets of the Gunpowder Plot.

▲ *The search was carried out by the flickering light of lanterns like this.*

▶ Documents like Guy Fawkes's confession can help us uncover the secrets of the plot.

◀ Thirty-six barrels of gunpowder would have exploded with devastating force if the plot had not been discovered.

CATHOLIC CONSPIRACY

The real name of the man arrested on 5 November 1605 was Guy Fawkes. Fawkes was just one member of a gang of plotters who had sworn a solemn oath to kill the King. The plotters were all followers of the Catholic religion. Their anger came from the bitter split between Catholic and Protestant Christians. This split occurred many years before the plot's discovery.

▲ This is the Great Seal of Henry VIII, used to seal important documents. Henry's break with the Pope was one of the turning points of English history.

For almost 100 years, Europe, including England and Scotland, had been torn apart by bitter religious arguments between different branches of the Christian church. Some countries chose to follow new Protestant beliefs. Elsewhere, the Catholic Church remained strong. Both sides believed that only they were right, and that the other side were heretics or enemies of true religion who must be defeated.

England had broken away from the Catholic Church in the 1530s, when Henry VIII was king. However, many people in England stuck to their Catholic beliefs. These Catholics included some of the most powerful people in the land. They were prepared to fight for what they believed in.

◀ King Henry VIII ruled England from 1509 to 1547. He broke with the Catholic Church after the Pope would not allow Henry to divorce his first wife.

▲ Both Protestants and Catholics were burned at the stake for their beliefs.

▼ Henry VIII closed Catholic monasteries and seized their wealth after his split from the Catholic Church.

▲ These notes were written by Sir Edward Coke, who questioned Fawkes after his arrest. Fawkes refused to reveal the names of his fellow plotters but Coke was sure that a "great man" was behind such an ambitious scheme aimed at the centre of English power.

HIDING THEIR FAITH

The Gunpowder Plotters had all suffered as Catholics during the long reign of Elizabeth I. Elizabeth tried to reach a compromise between Protestants and Catholics but, in 1570, the Pope declared that English Catholics could rise up against the Protestant Elizabeth.

Now all Catholics in England might be traitors, plotting to depose or even murder the Queen. New laws were passed. Fines were increased for Catholics who refused to attend services at their local Protestant parish church. These Catholics were called recusants.

▲ *The homes of Catholic nobles contained hidden rooms called priest holes to hide priests from the authorities.*

Catholics who sheltered priests or tried to convert others to their religion faced prison or even death. The Catholic religion became secret, with priests hidden in the houses of wealthy Catholics.

This was the world in which young Catholics such as Guy Fawkes grew up. They had to choose between loyalty to the English crown, and loyalty to their deepest beliefs.

▶ *Pope Pius V hands a messenger a decree of Elizabeth's excommunication.*

▼ This lodge was built by leading Catholic Thomas Tresham. It is covered with symbols to show his Catholic faith. Tresham's son Francis was one of the Gunpowder Plotters.

A government proclamation claimed that the Spanish Armada, which was sent to try and invade England in 1588, was all for the "relief and comfort" of England's Catholics, who it says were actually "traitors".

REBELLION AND REVOLT

The Gunpowder Plot was not the first attempt to murder an English monarch. Elizabeth I was constantly under threat from plots and rebellions, both from her own subjects and her enemies abroad.

Many Catholics believed that Elizabeth's cousin Mary Queen of Scots was the true queen of England. This was because the Catholic Church claimed that Henry VIII's marriage to Elizabeth's mother Anne Boleyn was illegal, so Elizabeth was not the rightful queen. Elizabeth kept Mary captive in England for nearly 20 years, after she was forced to leave Scotland. When coded letters were found linking Mary to a Catholic plot against Elizabeth, the Queen ordered Mary's execution on 8 February 1587.

▲ As long as Mary Queen of Scots was alive, she was a threat to Queen Elizabeth.

Foreign threat

At the same time Protestants and Catholics were battling for power in France and the Netherlands, which was ruled by Spain. Guy Fawkes himself fought on the Spanish side in this revolt. The Spanish Armada of 1588 was an attempt to make England Catholic again. It failed, but Catholic plotters believed that foreign powers would help them in their rebellion.

Essex executed

In 1601, Elizabeth's former favourite the Earl of Essex tried to raise a rebellion. Essex was executed but many of his Catholic supporters were spared, including Robert Catesby, the leader of the Gunpowder Plot.

◀ Mary Queen of Scots sent a coded letter to Anthony Babington, the leader of a plot against Elizabeth. Elizabeth's spies intercepted Mary's secret note and made this copy. Mary's fate was sealed.

▲ Catholic hopes were dashed once again when the English navy and fierce storms scattered the Spanish Armada.

Queen Elizabeth I

▲ Elizabeth I ruled England from 1558 to 1603.

New King, New Hope?

When Elizabeth died in 1603, Catholics in England hoped that things would get better. Elizabeth had no children to take over the crown and new King James was the son of a Catholic mother, Mary Queen of Scots. His wife Anne of Denmark was also a Catholic.

James had become King James VI of Protestant Scotland when he was just two years old. Once it was clear that James was likely to be the next king of England, Catholics looked for any sign of how their treatment would change.

The Earl of Northumberland, who may have been a secret Catholic, sent his relative Thomas Percy to Scotland. Percy's mission was to discover how James would treat Catholics. He returned with good news that James planned to allow much more freedom to Catholics. What Percy did not know was that James was promising similar things to Protestants. Not everyone could get what they wanted.

▲ *Catholics hoped that Queen Anne's Catholic faith would encourage the King to give them more freedom to worship.*

King James made Henry Percy, Earl of Northumberland the captain of his personal bodyguard. James insisted that the guards should swear allegiance to him, although the known Catholic Thomas Percy was one of them.

James I

Scottish suspicions

Queen Elizabeth's reign was a hard act to follow and the fact that James was Scottish did not help. Many of his new subjects distrusted their northern neighbours as much as they feared Catholic countries like Spain. James had to be careful before he changed anything.

▲ When King James VI of Scotland became James I of England, he was the first monarch to rule both Scotland and England.

◄ Scotland's capital Edinburgh was several days' journey from London. England's new ruler would be almost unknown to his new subjects.

13

HOPES DASHED

King James had been haunted by plots all his life. He was just a baby when his mother Mary was accused of murdering his father. He had been kidnapped by a gang of nobles at the age of 11 and faced constant threats as a teenager. James hoped that he would be safer as King of England than among the feuding nobles of Scotland.

At first, the signs were good. The prayers of Catholics seemed to be answered when James stopped fining recusants for not going to Protestant churches. Catholics could now worship in peace, but some people would only be happy when England was Catholic again.

Early attacks

The discovery of two plots against him in July 1603 showed James that life in England would not be so easy. The plotters were not all Catholics, and in fact it was Catholic priests that had alerted the authorities. But Catholics were involved and these plots put all Catholics under suspicion. These discovered plots made it much less likely that Catholics would get a better deal from the new king. Early in 1604, James announced his "utter detestation" of Catholics.

▲ In 1603, leading nobles were persuaded to support the Catholic cause at the royal court, in exchange for gold from Spain.

▶ The playwright William Shakespeare's father was probably Catholic, and Shakespeare himself may have had connections to Catholic families and even the Gunpowder Plotters themselves.

▶ James was a very religious man. In 1604, he ordered a new translation of the Bible to be made for the Church of England.

Mr. WILLIAM SHAKESPEARES
COMEDIES, HISTORIES, & TRAGEDIES.

Published according to the True Originall Copies.

LONDON
Printed by Isaac Iaggard, and Ed. Blount. 1623.

What was James's view of Catholics?

Many Catholics believed that James would give them freedom to worship. However, in February 1604, a new proclamation ordered all priests to leave the country. Fines for recusants would still be collected.

▶ Explorer and writer Sir Walter Raleigh was arrested and imprisoned in the Tower of London for his part in an early plot against the King.

A PLOT BEGINS

Most Catholics accepted that they would have to carry on their religion in secret. But for some, James's change of attitude was the last straw. If the king would not give them religious freedom, then they would find a way of removing him so they could have their way.

▲ *The plotters made their solemn promise on a prayer book to carry out their plan.*

On 20 May 1604, a small group of men met at the Duck and Drake inn, in a fashionable part of London. The meeting had been called by Robert Catesby, a popular leader who inspired those around him. His companions were Tom Wintour, John Wright, Thomas Percy and Guy Fawkes.

Catesby explained his simple but horrifying plan. The plot was to create a massive explosion beneath the Houses of Parliament in Westminster. The King would certainly be killed, along with his ministers and countless others including members of his family. In the chaos that followed, the plotters planned to put one of James's surviving children on the throne, and force them to declare a Catholic England. In a locked room, the Gunpowder Plotters swore a solemn oath to carry out their terrible plan.

▲ *Robert Catesby had been a wild young man but, by 1604, was devoutly religious.*

▲ A busy London inn was a normal place for a group of men to meet for business or entertainment.

◄ *The plotters thought that King James's nine-year-old daugther, Princess Elizabeth would help create a Catholic country if they made her queen.*

"He told me the nature of the disease required so sharp a remedy, and asked me if I would give my consent. I told him yes, … if he resolved upon it, I would venture my life …"

Tom Wintour remembers the first meeting and Catesby's powers of persuasion, from his later confession.

THE PLOTTERS

The five men who met at the Duck and Drake were bound by friendship and family ties as well as religion.

Although Guy Fawkes is the most famous of the plotters, Robert Catesby was the unchallenged leader. The plot was his idea and, when things got tough, it was Catesby's strength and inspiring personality that persuaded the others that their plan could be successful.

The plot widens

As the plot gathered pace, Catesby and others recruited more accomplices. The final 13 plotters included family members, such as Tom Wintour's brother Robert and rich friends Sir Everard Digby and Francis Tresham, who could provide, money, safe houses and horses.

▲ When in London, Catesby would meet his friends in inns such as the Mermaid, which was also popular with writers and actors.

Thomas Bates

Robert Wintour

Christopher Wright

John Wright

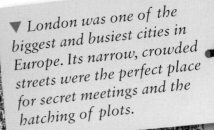

▼ London was one of the biggest and busiest cities in Europe. Its narrow, crowded streets were the perfect place for secret meetings and the hatching of plots.

John Wright *had fought alongside Catesby in the Essex rebellion. He was renowned as a man of action and a brilliant swordsman, as well as a devout Catholic.*

Thomas Percy *was a hot-headed young noble, committed to action for the Catholic cause. He had connections to the powerful Earl of Northumberland and was even a member of the King's bodyguard.*

Robert Catesby *was from a wealthy family but he chose life as a rebel. He was well known to the authorities and had been in prison for his part in the Earl of Essex's failed rebellion against Elizabeth I.*

Tom Wintour *was related to Catesby and fiercely loyal. He provided brains and connections. He had spent many years fighting abroad and his job was to try and recruit help from Catholic Spain.*

Thomas Percy

Guido (Guy) Fawkes

Robert Catesby

Tom Wintour

GUY FAWKES

Guy Fawkes was part of the plot from the start. Unlike many of the other plotters, Fawkes was almost unknown to government spies. He could put the bold plan into action without being watched. Even when he was arrested, investigators did not know his true identity.

Guy Fawkes was born in York in 1570. He grew up in a Protestant family until his father died when Fawkes was just eight years old. His mother married a Catholic and Fawkes was sent to a secretly Catholic school.

Fighting for his beliefs

When he was 21, Fawkes went to fight for Catholic Spain against the Protestant revolt in the Netherlands. It was in this bloody war that he became a skilled and respected soldier. He also met and impressed fellow soldier Tom Wintour.

▲ *The war between Dutch Protestants and their Spanish Catholic rulers was especially brutal.*

In 1603, Fawkes travelled to Spain. He wanted Spanish help in removing the new King James from England's throne. His request was refused. Soon after, Spain agreed a peace treaty with England, ending all hopes that the country would support the plot.

◀ *York's Catholic community was small but stubborn. Many recusants were imprisoned during Guy Fawkes's childhood in the city.*

◀ It was natural for Fawkes and others to look to European neighbours, including Spain, to help England's Catholics.

▼ This illustration showed that Guy Fawkes was tall, muscular and a highly trained soldier.

Fawkes had a strong dislike of the Scots. When trying to persuade Spain to support the fight against Scottish King James, he wrote:

"Even were there but one religion in England, it will not be possible to reconcile these two nations [England and Scotland], as they are, for very long."

He meant that the two countries could never be united under one ruler, even without the arguments over religion.

THE PLOT TAKES SHAPE

The plotters believed that the destruction of King James and his ministers would lead to a popular uprising. Catholics who had remained hidden would finally be free to support the rebels.

And so, in late May 1604, Catesby and his secret band put the first steps of the plan into action. They rented a house in the heart of Westminster, next to Parliament. From here, they could launch a devastating attack. They would later rent a cellar or storeroom beneath the House of Lords itself. The original plotters were joined by Robert Keyes, Kit Wright, Robert Wintour, John Grant and Catesby's servant Thomas Bates.

A setback

Everything had to be ready for the opening of Parliament in February 1605. All seemed to be going well until their plans were thrown into turmoil. An outbreak of the dreaded plague meant that this grand ceremony was delayed until the autumn. The plotters would have to keep their plan secret for months longer, and there was a risk that their gunpowder would decay and become useless.

▲ London was hit by regular and deadly plague epidemics. Public life was disrupted as the rich and powerful fled to their country homes.

◀ In 1605 there were houses and cellars all around the Parliament buildings. The current Houses of Parliament were built after a fire in 1834.

LONDINVM FERACISSIMI AN-GLIAE REGNI METROPOLIS

THE TOWRE

▼ In 1604 the plotters could transport their gunpowder to the heart of government along the busy River Thames.

Henry Ferrers.

▲ This is the lease that the plotters agreed for the house in the heart of Westminster, from where the explosion could be launched. The house was rented in the name of Thomas Percy.

Tunnel teaser?

The authorities claimed that the plotters spent many months digging a tunnel so the blast would explode directly beneath Parliament. This mine has never been found. It was probably invented to convince people that the explosion was designed to kill as many innocent people as possible.

SPIES AND SECRET POLICE

Keeping the plot secret was not easy when faced with the network of spies and informers controlled by the Secretary of State Robert Cecil, the Earl of Salisbury.

Cecil gathered information and reports from spies across Europe. They included priests who reported on the actions and contacts of Catholics abroad. Other agents investigated the plans of foreign countries. Spies passed on secrets in the hope of getting favours from the government themselves. Double agents worked for more than one country, selling their secrets to whoever paid them the most.

In 1605, Fawkes travelled to the Netherlands again in a last plea for Spanish help. A spy called Captain William Turner reported to Cecil that Fawkes would travel secretly to England to meet Catesby.

Turner did not know the details of the plot, or that Fawkes was using the name John Johnson. The report was just one of many plans that Cecil would have heard about, most of which came to nothing.

▲ Many historians think Robert Cecil knew more about the Gunpowder Plot than he ever admitted.

▼ With no phones or other ways of communicating, Cecil's spies filed their reports by letter or in person.

▼ Cecil's spies kept a close eye on ships travelling between England and mainland Europe.

Who knew what?

Cecil and the government may have known much more about the plot than they ever revealed. Even if the plotters all kept their oath of secrecy, some details could have been revealed by family members, servants, or even priests.

▶ Some spies would work for any country if the price was right.

▼ The plotters were careful to avoid writing to each other about their plan as letters could be intercepted and forged.

PLANNING THE ESCAPE ROUTE

Blowing up the Houses of Parliament would throw the country into chaos, but it would only be the start. What happened after the explosion was just as important to Catesby and his men.

Catesby decided that he needed more supporters to be sure of success. Ambrose Rookwood was a rich young Catholic who could bring a stable of swift horses. These would help the plotters to evade capture. Sir Everard Digby was also able to provide horses and money. Francis Tresham was Catesby's cousin by marriage and came from a well-known Catholic family.

▲ *Ambrose Rookwood paid for the gunpowder that would be used by the plotters, although he believed at the time that it was for English Catholics fighting in the Netherlands.*

Escape and kidnap

Fawkes had the vital job of setting off the giant explosion. In the confusion, he would escape across the sea to mainland Europe. It would be down to Catesby and the other conspirators to carry out the next stages of the plot. They would lead an uprising from several 'safe' houses in the Midlands and arrange the capture of King James's daughter Princess Elizabeth. The successful plotters would force Elizabeth to become queen of a new Catholic England.

▼ *Guy Fawkes would try to find safety in Catholic countries overseas.*

Princess Elizabeth

Who would rule after the plot?

Catesby planned to make Princess Elizabeth the new queen. But she was only nine years old. A leading lord would probably have become Lord Protector until she was old enough to rule alone. The plotters claimed that they would have chosen someone from the lords who survived the explosion, but this may have been a lie in order to protect the identity of their secret leader.

▼ Fast and strong horses would be essential as the plotters spread out across the country. John Grant was in charge of raiding the stables at Warwick Castle after the explosion.

THE FATAL LETTER

With just a month to go until the fateful night, rumours started to circulate among Catholics – something big was about to happen. People close to the plotters may have known more than they ever admitted.

Lord Monteagle was a leading Catholic. He had been involved in Essex's rebellion during the time of Queen Elizabeth, but had always been loyal to King James. On 26 October he was eating dinner with guests when a letter was delivered. Monteagle asked a servant to read the letter aloud. What he heard was a terrible blow for the plot.

The letter warned Monteagle not to go to the opening of Parliament on 5 November. Monteagle immediately passed the information to the King's chief minister Robert Cecil. Cecil's reaction was to wait and see what happened. This was the chance for the plotters to save themselves.

"... I would advise you ... to devise some excuse to shift of your attendance at this Parliament; for God and man have concurred to punish the wickedness of this time."

The warning delivered to Lord Monteagle.

Who wrote the letter?

People at the time believed the letter was written by Francis Tresham to warn his friend, but was there more to it than that? Could the letter have been written by someone who wished to end the plot? Monteagle himself may have known something was up, as a leading Catholic. It may even have been written by Cecil or one of his spies as a way of exposing a plot they had already discovered.

▼ Francis Tresham always denied writing the letter, although he was accused by Catesby.

◄ We may never know for sure who wrote it, but the Monteagle letter was a disaster for the plotters. The actual letter still survives in the National Archives in England.

FINAL PREPARATIONS

When they learned of the letter at least one of the plotters tried to persuade Catesby to abandon the scheme. Surely it would be too risky now? Catesby argued that the authorities knew no details of the plot, apart from the day and that Parliament was the target. Recklessly, the plotters acted as if nothing had happened.

▼ *Fawkes was worried that some gunpowder had decayed and may not explode, so extra barrels were added.*

Tresham's escape plan

Francis Tresham tried to persuade Catesby to stop the explosion. On 2 November he gained a written passport allowing himself and two others to leave England. Was this a desperate escape plan?

▼ *The conspirators stashed muskets and ammunition for the battles to come.*

In the few days before 5 November, Guy Fawkes checked that the gunpowder was all in place beneath the Houses of Parliament. His comrades took up their positions. Ambrose Rookwood, Robert Keyes and Tom Wintour were stationed in London. Thomas Percy also returned to the capital after visiting his powerful family to discover how much the authorities knew of the plot.

The hunting party

On 4 November, Sir Everard Digby organized a 'hunting party', just a few miles from where Princess Elizabeth was staying. He was joined by a group of Catholic friends, who probably knew nothing of the plan to kidnap Elizabeth. Meanwhile, Catesby, Bates and John Wright were leaving London. Their job was to start a rebellion in the Midlands once Parliament and the King were destroyed.

▲ Sir Everard Digby was the last plotter to be recruited.

▲ Thomas Percy visited the Earl of Northumberland at Syon House on 4 November. His visit meant that Northumberland was later imprisoned for being involved in the plot.

▼ Hunting was a common pastime in 1605, so a hunting party was a good way of hiding Digby's true plan to kidnap Princess Elizabeth.

THE PLOT UNRAVELS

▲ *This engraving shows the Eye of Heaven condemning Guy Fawkes as he approaches Parliament.*

As Guy Fawkes and the other conspirators prepared for their glorious rebellion, King James and the Earl of Salisbury were planning their own next steps. The King had seen the letter sent to Monteagle, but he and his chief minister chose to take no action until the night before the opening of Parliament.

On the afternoon of 4 November, the Lord Chamberlain made a quick search of Parliament, the cellar beneath it and the surrounding buildings. He noticed a large pile of firewood in a cellar and a tall, bearded servant.

They discovered that the firewood belonged to a small house rented by the well-known Catholic, Thomas Percy. Why was there such a large pile of firewood for such a small house? At midnight, they returned and arrested the man they thought was Percy's servant. He was in fact Guy Fawkes, using the name John Johnson. The searchers also discovered 36 barrels of gunpowder, enough to destroy Parliament and everyone in it.

An entry in the House of Commons journal for 5 November 1605 records the arrest of
"one Johnson, servant to Mr Thomas Percy, ... who had placed 36 barrels of gunpowder in the vault under the House, with a purpose to blow King and the whole Company, when they should there assemble".

▶ *The cellar of the House of Lords as it would have looked in 1605.*

▲ *Guy Fawkes was a skilled soldier who would not give himself up without a fight.*

Why did they wait?

If the government knew about the plot from the Monteagle letter, why did they wait until the last minute before searching Parliament? Maybe they thought that waiting longer would give them more chance to catch the plotters, or maybe they knew the details of the plot and were not worried about it.

THE HUNTERS HUNTED

Within a few hours, news reached the conspirators in London that Fawkes had been caught and there would be no explosion. But the plotters had spread out across the country. Only Thomas Percy's name had been linked to the plot. Could the others escape capture?

Tom Wintour stayed in London for several hours, gathering details of what was known. The other plotters fled as fast as their horses could carry them. Ambrose Rookwood was one of the last to leave. Rookwood was a skilled horseman and quickly caught up with the others. Catesby, Percy, Bates, the Wright brothers, and Rookwood rode on into Warwickshire in central England. They knew their only hope was to escape or die trying.

Celebration and confusion

In London, as the news of the plot spread, bonfires were being lit to celebrate the King's narrow escape. But the lords who were also targets of the explosion were in a confused state. It was still not clear who the plotters were. No one knew which lords might be involved in this terrible crime.

▶ *Immediately after the discovery of the plot, the government issued this proclamation calling for the arrest of Thomas Percy "by all possible means, especially to keep him alive, … [so that] the rest of the Conspirators may be discovered."*

▶ *Catesby reached his family home at Ashby-St-Ledgers in Northamptonshire on the evening of 5 November. He met Robert Wintour in the fields and told him about the plot's discovery.*

▲ Thomas Percy was linked to the plot because his name had been used to rent the house near Parliament.

▲ The plot's failure was a disaster for the plotters themselves, but also for their families and servants who may have known some details.

INTERROGATION AND TORTURE

As the plotters fled from London, their hopes rested on Guy Fawkes. The battle-hardened soldier would be under extreme pressure to reveal their names. How long would it be before he cracked?

After his arrest, 'John Johnson' was taken to the King's private rooms for questioning, before being imprisoned in the feared Tower of London. For almost two days he revealed nothing about the other plotters, although he admitted his plan to blow up Parliament. On 6 November, King James ordered 'Johnson' to be tortured to find the truth.

Torture methods used in the Tower of London included the manacles. The prisoner would be hung from a wall by metal bands around his wrists. If this did not work they would use the rack. This was the most feared device and was used to stretch the prisoner's body until he confessed. Fawkes managed to hold out until 7 November, but finally he talked.

▼ Fawkes signed two confessions; one after torture and one a few days later. The effects of his ordeal can be seen in the spidery, shaky signature below.

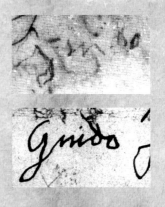

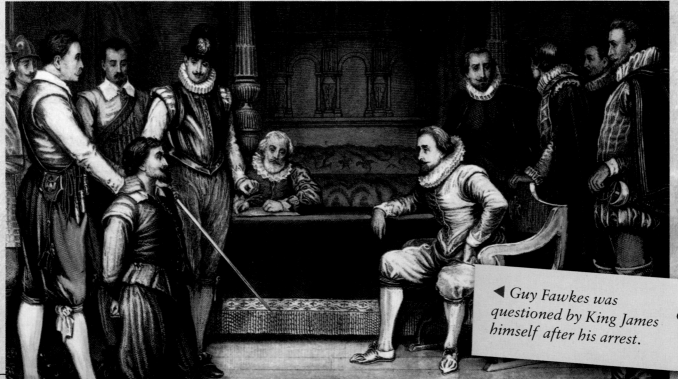

◀ Guy Fawkes was questioned by King James himself after his arrest.

▼ The Tower of London was both a royal palace and dreaded prison. Many of the plotters spent time in its dungeons.

Evidence under pressure

Use of torture is one reason why we can't be sure of some details of the plot. To end their torment, prisoners would often say what their captors wanted to hear, whether it was true or not.

◄ The King himself drew up a list of questions for Guy Fawkes to answer, beginning with finding out "as to what he is, for I can never yet hear of any man that knows him".

this examinate wolde now be maid to ansoure to fo

1   as quhat he is, for I can never yett heare of any

2   quhaire he was borne,

3   quhat waire his parents names,

4   quhat aage he is of,

5   quhaire he hath liued,

6   hou he hath liued & by quhat trade of lyfe,

7   hou he ressaued those woundes in his breste,   & hou long

8   if he was euer in seruice with any other before percie, & quhat they wa

9   hou came he in percies seruice, by quhat meanes, & at quhat tyme

10 quhat tyme was this house hyred by his maister,   preparatio

11 & hou soone after the possessing of it did he beginne to his deuillishe

12 quhen & quhaire lernid he to speake frenshe,

13 quhat gentle womans lettir it was that was founde upon him,   to him

14 & quhair for doth sho giue him an other name in it then he giue

15 if he was euer a papiste, & if so quho broche him up in it

16 if other wayes, hou was he converted, quhaire, quhen, & quho

this course of his lyfe same the more desirouse to & now becaus

I haue dyuers motiues leading me to suspecte that he hath remain

long beyonde the seas & ather is a preiste, or hath long seruid

SHOWDOWN AT HOLBEACH HOUSE

Even though there would be no explosion at Parliament, and Guy Fawkes was a prisoner, Catesby refused to believe the plot was finished. If ordinary Catholics could rise up against the King, maybe they could still win. They just needed time to plan the fightback.

▲ *Coughton Court was a refuge for many Catholics, including priests. Catesby sent Thomas Bates to Coughton to warn these people that they were all in terrible danger.*

▲ *Robert Catesby died before he could reveal many secrets of the Gunpowder Plot.*

Catesby rode on with a small band of followers. They raided Warwick Castle for fresh horses and weapons. By this time, the government was on their trail, although Fawkes had still not revealed their names.

Fight to the death

As the small band got further from London they hoped more followers would join them. However, even family and friends turned against them. They finally arrived at Holbeach House in Worcestershire, where they would stand and fight. They were soon faced with 200 soldiers led by the High Sheriff of Worcestershire. It was an uneven fight and no one wanted to be taken prisoner. Percy, Jack and Kit Wright and Catesby himself were killed in the struggle to escape. Tom Wintour, Grant and Rookwood were taken alive.

◀ *By 7 November, the government had a good idea of who the traitors were. This proclamation called for the arrest of Percy and other plotters.*

▲ Most of the plotters came from the rural midlands and they hoped to find a safe hiding place there.

Dangerous decision

Their gunpowder was soaked by heavy rain and the exhausted plotters unwisely decided to dry it by the fire. A spark from the fire set off an explosion that injured Catesby, John Grant and Rookwood.

▲ Tom Wintour's later confession described his arrival at Holbeach House, where he met Catesby: "When I came I found Mr. Catesby reasonable well, Mr. Percy, both the Wrights, Mr. Rokewood and Mr. Grant. I asked them what they resolved to do. They answered "We mean here to die". I said again I would take such part as they did."

FINDING THE GUILTY

▲ *Playwright Ben Jonson was Catholic, a known troublemaker and shared a name with "John Johnson" (Guy Fawkes). It is no surprise that he fell under suspicion.*

A few days after the failed explosion, most of the plotters were either dead or imprisoned. The government now turned its attention to catching anyone else who had known of the disastrous plan.

The remaining plotters were soon rounded up. Robert Wintour was the last to be arrested in December. Several lords with family or other connections to the plotters were also sent to the Tower of London. Well-known Catholics rushed to deny all knowledge of the plot, and to share what little they knew or guessed with the government.

The search widens

The plotters were connected to many of England's leading Catholic families and the Jesuit priests they sheltered. Thomas Bates confessed that he had discussed the plot with a priest and soon the whole Catholic community was suspected. Priests were forced to go into hiding or flee abroad.

◀ *Lawyer and philosopher Francis Bacon was strongly anti-Catholic and helped to investigate the Gunpowder Plot.*

▼ Thomas Percy's treason was a disaster for the Percy family, whose ancestral home was Alnwick Castle in Northumberland.

Who was in charge?

Salisbury was sure that one of the country's leading nobles was behind the plot. The Earl of Northumberland was imprisoned because of his links to Thomas Percy. If Catesby had lived, he may have revealed whether there really was a powerful supporter behind the plot.

▼ The authorities were desperate to find a link between the plot and Jesuit priests such as Henry Garnet.

◄ Not all the names supplied by informers were actually involved. This list includes many guilty men and some, such as playwright Ben Jonson, who were not involved.

Si quid patimini propter iustitiam, beati i. petri Henricus Garnetus anglus e societate IESV passus

· 3· May · 1606·   IOHAN · WIERICX · F · EXCVD · CVM · G · ET · PRIVILL · SIG · D · BVSCHER ·

TRIAL AND PUNISHMENT

Some might say the plotters who had been killed in the battle at Holbeach House were the lucky ones. The others were held in terrible conditions in the Tower of London. Some may have been tortured as their captors tried to prove that priests and known enemies of the government had been part of the plot.

The trials began on 27 January 1606. Francis Tresham had already died of illness in December. It did not take long to find the eight surviving plotters guilty of high treason. They were left in no doubt about the horrible fate that awaited them.

Powder problem

The 36 barrels of gunpowder found beneath Parliament were described as "decayed" because they had been stored too long. They may not even have exploded if Fawkes had managed to light the fuse.

◄ *The conspirators were tried in a packed Westminster Hall.*

▼ *There was no chance that the traitors would be found not guilty, and no lawyers argued in their favour.*

42

Crowds gathered for the grisly executions despite the fact that they were carried out early in the morning in January.

A traitor's death

The penalty for high treason was to be hung, drawn and quartered. The guilty men would be hanged by the neck until half dead, then their bowels and heart would be removed, and finally their heads would be severed and their bodies cut into pieces. The whole grisly event would attract a large crowd.

The first four plotters suffered this terrible punishment on 30 January 1606. The remaining four were executed the following day. Guy Fawkes was the last to climb the fatal scaffold.

Guy Fawkes's head was placed on a spike on London Bridge, as a warning to other traitors.

FACT AND FICTION

We know the story of the Gunpowder Plot from the many written records that have survived. Documents such as the confessions of Fawkes and Wintour and official proclamations can be used by writers and historians to piece together the events of 1605.

But many mysteries of the plot remain unsolved. Robert Catesby never lived to tell his side of the story. We know that Guy Fawkes's confession was probably gained using torture, meaning that he would say almost anything to end his ordeal. Tom Wintour's confession may be a similar story. His signature was probably forged.

A plot that never was?

Some people have even suggested that the plot itself was invented by Robert Cecil, Earl of Salisbury, as a way to silence England's Catholics. Was Catesby persuaded by secret government agents to launch the plot? Such an idea can never be proved, but the plot certainly had a dramatic effect on the Catholic community.

▲ The confessions of Guy Fawkes and Tom Wintour were published with other documents in the King's Book. This became the official story of the Gunpowder Plot.

▶ One of the biggest mysteries is the letter to Lord Monteagle. Who wrote it? Was it Monteagle himself to make clear that he was not involved? The paper has been tested and we now know it came from the Netherlands. Many of the plotters had links in this area, but so did government agents.

114

6

▲ At his trial, Wintour blamed himself for involving his brother Robert in the plot. He begged for Robert's life to be spared.

◀ Can Tom Wintour's confession be trusted? The signature on it was different from any other signature by Wintour that has survived. He had also been shot in the arm during the siege at Holbeach House so may not even have been able to sign his name.

CATHOLIC CALAMITY

The plotters themselves paid a terrible price for their actions, but the plot was a disaster for all Catholics in England. One of the most prominent Catholics to be dragged into the plot was Father Henry Garnet, the leader of England's Jesuits.

Father Garnet's fate

Garnet went into hiding after the plot was discovered. He and another priest hid in a tiny priest hole until 27 January before they gave themselves up. Garnet's crime was that he knew some details of the plot but had not revealed them to the authorities. He shared the same fate as the plotters and was hung, drawn and quartered on 3 May 1606.

Catholics in crisis

The disastrous plot plunged England's Catholics into crisis for hundreds of years. New laws stopped Catholics from voting in elections and practicing law. In 1613, there were even attempts to force Catholics to wear red hats in public. There were regular rumours of Catholic plots and they were blamed for many disasters, including the Great Fire of London.

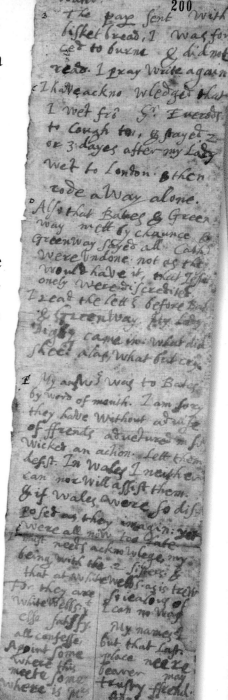

◀ Catholic worship was even more restricted after the plot, with Catholics forced to marry in Protestant churches.

▲ Garnet wrote secret letters from his prison cell. Warming this letter revealed Garnet's words, written in orange juice. The letters were read by Garnet's jailers so never reached their intended readers.

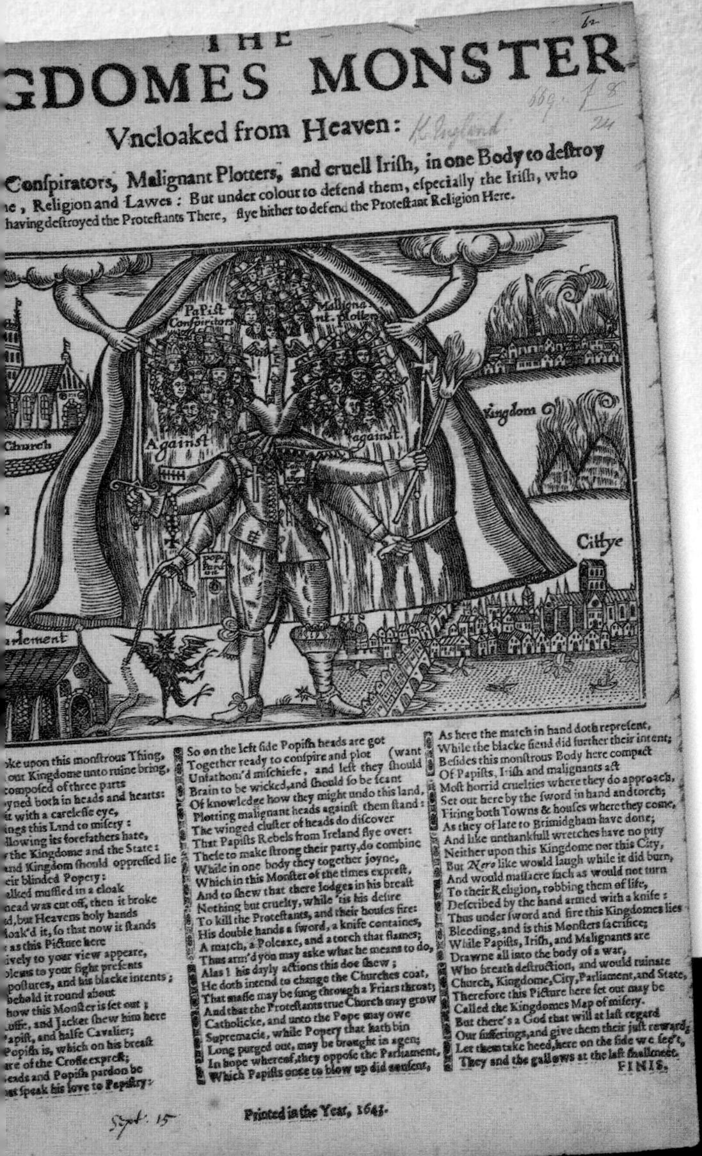

THE
GDOMES MONSTER
Vncloaked from Heaven:
Conspirators, Malignant Plotters, and cruell Irish, in one Body to destroy
ne, Religion and Lawes: But under colour to defend them, especially the Irish, who
having destroyed the Protestants There, flye hither to defend the Protestant Religion Here.

oke upon this monstrous Thing,
our Kingdome unto ruine bring,
composed of three parts
oyned both in heads and hearts:
it with a carelesse eye,
ings this Land to misery:
llowing its forefathers hate,
the Kingdome and the State:
and Kingdom should oppressed lie
eir blinded Popery:
alked muffled in a cloak
ead was cut off, then it broke
ad, but Heavens holy hands
loak'd it, so that now it stands
as this Picture here
ively to your view appeare,
pleases to your sight presents
postures, and his blacke intents;
behold it round about
how this Monster is set out;
uffe, and Jacket shew him here
Papist, and halfe Cavalier;
Popish is, which on his breast
are of the Crosse exprest;
eads and Popish pardon be
st speak his love to Papistry:

So on the left side Popish heads are got
Together ready to conspire and plot (want
Unfathom'd mischiefe, and lest they should
Brain to be wicked, and should so be scant
Of knowledge how they might undo this land,
Plotting malignant heads against them stand:
The winged cluster of heads do discover
That Papists Rebels from Ireland flye over:
These to make strong their party, do combine
While in one body they together joyne,
Which in this Monster of the times exprest,
And to shew that there lodges in his breast
Nothing but cruelty, while 'tis his desire
To kill the Protestants, and their houses fire:
His double hands a sword, a knife containes,
A match, a Poleaxe, and a torch that flames;
Thus arm'd you may aske what he means to do,
Alas! his dayly actions this doe shew;
He doth intend to change the Churches coat,
That masse may be sung through a Friars throat;
And that the Protestants true Church may grow
Catholicke, and unto the Pope may owe
Supremacie, while Popery that hath bin
Long purged out, may be brought in agen;
In hope whereof, they oppose the Parliament,
Which Papists once to blow up did consent,

As here the match in hand doth represent,
While the blacke fiend did further their intent;
Besides this monstrous Body here compact
Of Papists, Irish and malignants act
Most horrid cruelties where they do approach,
Set out here by the sword in hand and torch;
Firing both Towns & houses where they come,
As they of late to Brimidgham have done;
And like unthankfull wretches have no pity
Neither upon this Kingdome nor this City,
But Nero like would laugh while it did burn,
And would massacre such as would not turn
To their Religion, robbing them of life,
Described by the hand armed with a knife:
Thus under sword and fire this Kingdomes lies
Bleeding, and is this Monsters sacrifice;
While Papists, Irish, and Malignants are
Drawne all into the body of a war,
Who breath destruction, and would ruinate
Church, Kingdome, City, Parliament, and State,
Therefore this Picture here set out may be
Called the Kingdomes Map of misery.
But there's a God that will at last regard
Our sufferings, and give them their just reward;
Let them take heed, here on the side we see't,
They and the gallows at the last shall meet.
FINIS.

Printed in the Year, 1643.

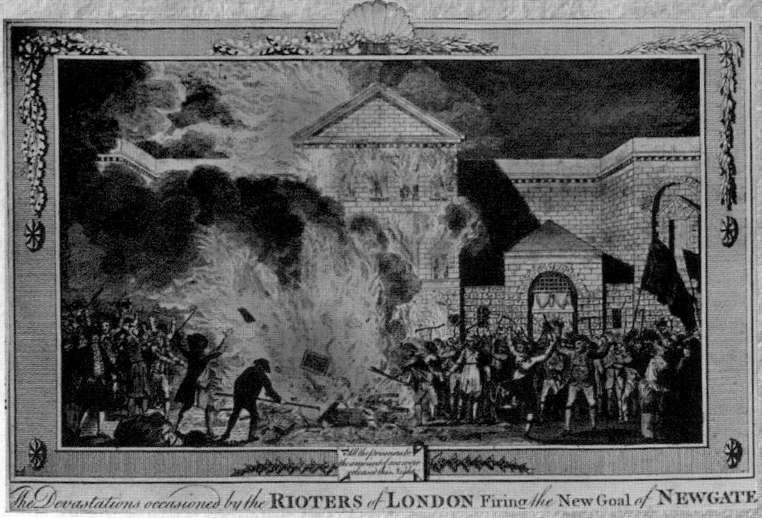

▲ *In 1780, London was torn apart by riots when some anti-Catholic laws were relaxed.*

◀ *An anti-Catholic pamphlet from 1643.*

▼ *When the Great Fire of London destroyed much of the city in 1666, Catholics were accused of starting the fire deliberately.*

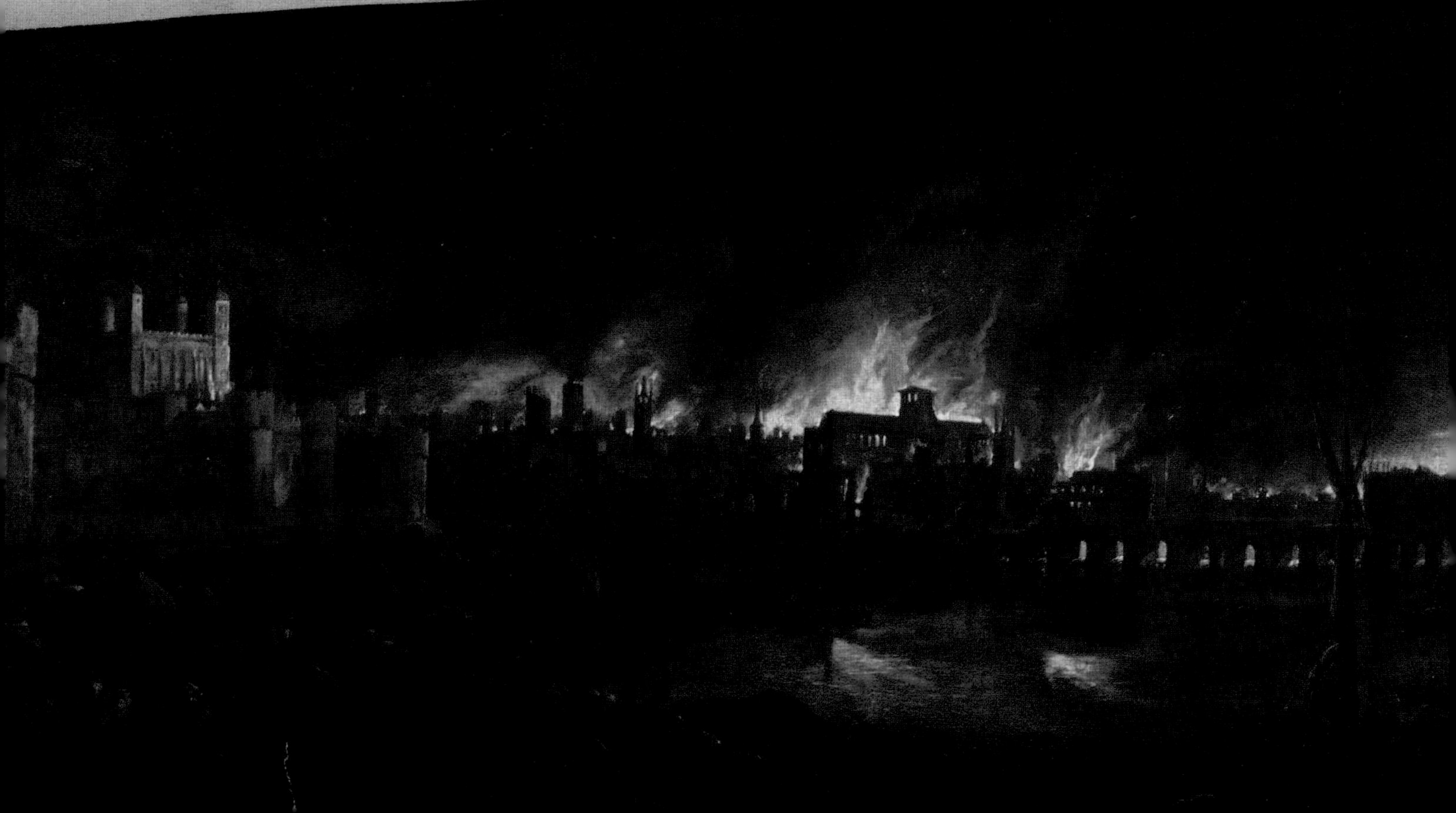

TURBULENT TIMES

The religious turmoil that caused the Gunpowder Plot did not end with the execution of the plotters. For a while the discovery of the plot, and the public outrage against those who had tried to kill the king, strengthened the position of Scottish King James on the English throne. However, within a few years Britain was plunged into some of the most turbulent times in its history.

▲ Less than 40 years after Catesby's failure, rival armies were fighting on British soil.

Civil war

Religious disputes still raged across Europe. In England and Scotland these disputes were mainly between different branches of Protestantism. As James's reign went on, divisions grew between the King and Parliament.

James's son King Charles I came to the throne in 1625. His arguments with Parliament, combined with religious divisions, led to civil wars across the British Isles. In 1649, Charles I was executed by Parliament, just a few metres from where the Gunpowder Plotters had planned to murder his father.

In many ways, the Gunpowder Plot was an early sign of battles to come throughout the 1600s. In 1688, King James II was forced to leave power because he was a Catholic. The people of Britain were not afraid to remove their monarchs if they disagreed with their beliefs.

Charles I

The future King Charles II used the hiding places built for Catholic priests to escape his enemies during the civil war.

In some churches, you can still see carvings and decorations that were damaged or destroyed by Puritans.

Charles I was beheaded on 30 January 1649, exactly 43 years after the first gunpowder plotters were executed.

Hard-line Puritan Protestants rather than Catholics succeeded in overthrowing and executing Charles I.

WHAT IF THE PLOT HAD SUCCEEDED?

Although Guy Fawkes was arrested just a few hours before the planned explosion, the plot only ever had a small chance of success. The letter to Lord Monteagle gave the government plenty of time to foil the plan, and they may even have known about it long before. How would history have been different if the dramatic explosion had happened on 5 November 1605?

▲ *The State Opening of Parliament still takes place every year.*

The country would have been thrown into chaos after such a terrible event, with King James and most of England's leading figures dead in the rubble of the Houses of Parliament. The plotters hoped that this would lead to a revolution of England's Catholics, but Protestants would not have given in so easily. The most likely outcome would probably have been a bloody civil war.

▲ *Catholics were not the only ones who wanted freedom to follow their religion. In 1620, a group of Protestants left 'ungodly' England and sailed to America on the Mayflower. They founded colonies that would eventually become the United States of America.*

Foreign invasion

Guy Fawkes and his comrades were hoping for help from Spain after the plot had succeeded. A foreign invasion could have changed Britain forever. Britain's system of government could have been swept away and English people could now be speaking Spanish rather than English. In many ways, modern Britain was shaped by the events of the 1600s, particularly the civil wars of the 1640s. If the Gunpowder Plot had succeeded, history would be very different.

▲ *Marie Antoinette and her husband King Louis XVI were executed after the French Revolution of 1789, which led to wars across Europe. The Gunpowder Plot could have had a similar effect.*

REMEMBER, REMEMBER, THE 5TH OF NOVEMBER

The date of the Gunpowder Plot has never been forgotten in Britain. Bonfires were lit in the streets of London on the day that the plot was discovered. In 1606, 5 November was made a day of thanksgiving by Parliament.

In the 1600s and 1700s, the anniversary was celebrated with bell-ringing and public bonfires. The festival was also strongly anti-Catholic. This changed in the 1800s when traditional firework and bonfire parties became more common.

▼ In the past, children made effigies of Guy Fawkes to burn on their bonfires.

Today, Bonfire Night is celebrated with organized firework displays and bonfires in towns across the UK. The tradition of burning a stuffed dummy called a 'guy' is much less popular than it was in the past. The festival now has fewer obvious links to the Gunpowder Plot of 1605.

◀ British people still spend hundreds of millions of pounds each year celebrating Bonfire Night.

Why do we still remember the plot?

The Gunpowder Plot has remained a national event because of the Act of Parliament that was passed in 1605 to make sure it was remembered. Special church services were held to celebrate the King's rescue from the plot.

▲ Most British towns organise an annual fireworks display on 5th November.

▼ The town of Lewes is home to a huge Bonfire Night festival every year, with thousands of people marching through the streets. Effigies, or dummies, of public figures such as politicians are often burned on the town's bonfires.

TREASON AND TERRORISM

Failed plots do not normally become as famous as the Gunpowder Plot did. Its fame rests on the annual celebration of Bonfire Night in the UK. More than 400 years after the plot, it can be difficult to understand why the desperate plotters acted as they did.

Religious freedom

In the modern world, it is widely accepted that people should be free to follow whatever religion they choose, although this is not true of every country. Catesby and his fellow plotters did not believe in religious freedom for all. They believed that they were right to use violence to force their beliefs on those they thought were heretics.

▲ *The noise and bright colours of Bonfire Night can make us forget what a terrible disaster the Gunpowder Plot could have been.*

Peaceful protest

People can often achieve their aims by peaceful protests or by voting for their leaders in a democratic system. The Gunpowder Plotters did not have this right. If they were going to take action, they saw rebellion as their only choice.

Even today, extreme groups still use an attack on a political leader as a way to get attention for their cause or to achieve what they want. Attacking political leaders often has the opposite effect as governments crack down against opponents. This was the reaction in the weeks after the Gunpowder Plot.

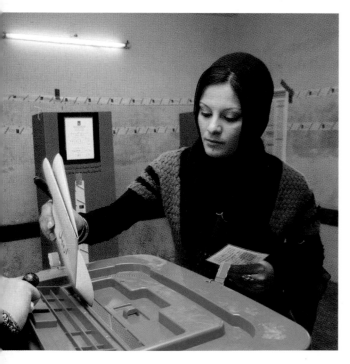

▲ *Voting in elections gives people a way to protest about their leaders.*

▲ *Today, we assume that all leaders need to have tight security.*

Terrorists use violence or threats to achieve their political aims, often working in small groups. The plotters were certainly planning a terrorist attack on the King and Parliament. Many English Catholics wanted to be free to follow their religion, they did not support the extreme tactics used by Catesby's men.

◄▼ *The murders of US President John F Kennedy and African-American leader Martin Luther King during the 1960s shocked the world, but the Gunpowder Plot shows that political violence is nothing new.*

LOOKING FOR CLUES

The Gunpowder Plot was planned in secret more than 400 years ago, but we know a lot about the plotters and their scheme. This is because many documents have survived from the time, such as the confession of Guy Fawkes himself. What other clues can we find today that tell us about England at the time of the plot?

The Houses of Parliament were rebuilt after a fire in 1834. Westminster Hall survives as the oldest part of the building. This was where the Gunpowder Plotters faced trial in 1606.

Every year before the State Opening of Parliament, royal bodyguards, known as Yeomen of the Guard or Beefeaters, search the Houses of Parliament for gunpowder. This tradition dates back to 1605.

GUY FAWKES

Hereabouts lived the parents of Guy Fawkes of Gunpowder Plot fame, who was baptized in St. Michael-le-Belfrey Church in 1570.

Many buildings linked to the plot have disappeared since 1605. Much of London was destroyed by the Great Fire of London in 1666 and the buildings where the plot was hatched are no longer standing. This plaque marks where Guy Fawkes's birthplace once stood in York.

GUNPOWDER PLOT TIMELINE

1558 Reign of Elizabeth I begins after the death of her Catholic sister Mary I.

1559 Acts of Uniformity and Supremacy require all citizens to attend Church of England services, with those who refuse being fined and called recusants.

1570 Elizabeth is excommunicated by the Catholic Pope, who allows Catholics to rise up and depose her.

8 February 1587 Mary Queen of Scots is executed for plotting against Elizabeth.

24 March 1603 Queen Elizabeth dies and is succeeded by King James I, who is already James VI of Scotland.

July 1603 Arrest of those involved in two plots against King James.

Guy Fawkes travels to Spain to seek help for a rebellion.

February 1604 Robert Catesby starts to make plans for the Gunpowder Plot. Tom Wintour travels to Flanders to recruit his friend Guy Fawkes.

20 May 1604 First meeting of the Gunpowder Plotters at the Duck and Drake Inn in London.

24 May 1604 Thomas Percy rents a small house from John Whynniard, close to the Houses of Parliament.

March 1605 Plotters rent a cellar or storeroom underneath the House of Lords.

26 October 1605 Lord Monteagle receives a letter warning him to stay away from the State Opening of Parliament.

4 November 1605 Sir Everard Digby meets friends for the 'hunting party' that was planned to kidnap Princess Elizabeth.

5 November 1605 (Just after midnight) Guy Fawkes is arrested and the gunpowder discovered. Bonfires are lit in London to celebrate the failure of the plot.

7 November 1605 Guy Fawkes confesses some details of the plot.

8 November 1605 Robert Catesby, Kit and John Wright and Thomas Percy are killed in a siege at Holbeach House, other plotters are arrested.

December 1605 Francis Tresham dies while imprisoned in the Tower of London.

27 January 1606 Trial of the eight surviving plotters.

30 January 1606 Execution of Sir Everard Digby, John Grant, Robert Wintour and Thomas Bates.

31 January 1606 Execution of Tom Wintour, Robert Keyes, Ambrose Rookwood and Guy Fawkes.

3 May 1606 Father Henry Garnet is executed for knowing about the plot but not informing the authorities.

Si quid patimini propter iustitiam, beati. 1. petri 3. Henricus Garnetus anglus e societate IESV passus 3. May. 1606.

GLOSSARY

Catholic Christian who is a member of the Roman Catholic Church, led by the pope

civil war conflict between two sides from the same country, to gain control of that country

conspirator someone who takes part in a plot or conspiracy

decree an official order that has the force of law

democratic based on the votes of all the people, such as a government chosen by voters in an election

depose removed from a position suddenly and forcefully

devout strictly religious

double agent spy who pretends to work for one country, while actually spying on behalf of another

effigy a model or sculpture of a person

evidence information that can help to prove something, such as whether a person has committed a crime

excommunitcate to exclude someone from church memebership

execute when a person is killed on the orders of a court because they have been found guilty of a crime

feud bitter and long-lasting disagreement or argument

government a group of people with the authority to rule

heretic person with religious beliefs that go against teaching of the main church

historian an expert (or student) in history, usually in a specific period of time

informer someone who passes on information about others to authorities

Jesuit member of the Society of Jesus, a group within the Roman Catholic Church who try to convert others to join the Church

lease agreement to rent a property

monarch king or queen

noble someone belonging to one of the country's most powerful and richest families

pamphlet small book without a hard cover or binding

Parliament the body that made laws in England in the 1600s, and now passes laws for the United Kingdom

persecution attack a particular person or group of people, especially for their race or beliefs

priest hole hidden room where priests could hide to escape capture

proclamation official document or announcement

Protestant Christian who is a member of any of the churches that broke away from the Roman Catholic Church from the 1500s onwards

Puritan group of Protestants who lived according to a strict religious code, seeing many pleasures and luxuries as sinful

rebellion an organised armed resistance to a government or ruler

recusant Catholic who refused to attend Protestant church services, which they were expected to do in Elizabethan England

revolution violent overthrow of a government or system to be replaced by something new

reign a period of time during which a monarch is in power

terrorist person or group of people who use violence against ordinary people to achieve a political goal

torture inflicting pain on someone as a punishment or so they give information about a crime

traitor someone who betrays a person, country or cause

treason betraying or committing a crime against your country or government

treaty agreement between two countries or organizations

turmoil a time of great disruption and confusion

Find out more

Books

The Gunpowder Plot by Ann Turnbull (A & C Black, 2014)

Guy Fawkes By Richard Brassey (Orion, 2005)

Horrible Histories: Slimy Stuarts by Terry Deary (Scholastic, 2007)

Ladybird Histories: Tudors and Stuarts (Ladybird, 2013)

Who Was Guy Fawkes? by Dereen Taylor (Wayland, 2009)

Gunpowder Plot: Terror and Faith in 1605 by Antonia Fraser (Weidenfeld and Nicolson, 1996) – the definitive account of the plot for older readers.

Online resources

The National Archives has created a lesson looking at some of the documents from the Gunpowder Plot:
www.nationalarchives.gov.uk/education/lesson07.htm

This website draws on parliamentary archives to tell the story of the plot:
www.parliament.uk/gunpowderplot/adults_index.htm

The BBC website includes lots of information and reconstructions of the plot
www.bbc.co.uk/history/the_gunpowder_plot

As well as this Gunpowder Plot game:
www.bbc.co.uk/history/british/civil_war_revolution/launch_gms_gunpowder_plot.shtml

Spartacus Educational's history website includes primary sources about the plot:
www.spartacus.schoolnet.co.uk/STUgunpowderP.htm

A short video exploring the men behind the Gunpowder Plot:
natgeotv.com/uk/the-gunpowder-plot/videos/historys-1st-terrorist-attack

A The National Archives

The National Archives is the UK government's official archive containing over 1,000 years of history. They give detailed guidance to government departments and the public sector on information management, and advise others about the care of historical archives.
www.nationalarchives.gov.uk

National Archives picture acknowledgements and catalogue references

p5 SP 14/216 doc54 (90v) Declaration of Guy Fawkes, p6 E 329/475 Great Seal of Henry VIII, p7 SP14/216/6 Edward Coke's notes on Fawkes initial interrogation, p10-11 SP 12/193 (54) and SP 53/18 (5) Babington postscript and cipher used with Mary Queen of Scots, p11 COPY 1/142 (ii) f320 Spanish Armada, p22 SP 14/216 (8) The lease of the house next to Parliament, p28-29 SP14/216/2 Warning letter to Lord Monteagle, p35 SP 14/73/67 or SP 14/16 doc 8 (18) Proclamation for the arrest of Thomas Percy, 5th November 1605, p36 SP 14/216 f152b and SP 14/216 doc54 (90v) two versions of Guy Fawkes signature, p37 SP 14/216 (34a) Interrogation questions and authorisation from James I, p38 SP 14/16 doc 20 (32) Proclamation for the arrest of Thomas Percy, 7th November 1605, p39 SP 14/216 Pt2 (10v) Thomas Wintour's Confession, 23rd of November 1605, p40 SP 14/216 (132) List of plotters supplied by informer, p41 SP 14/216 Pt2 (165a) Father Henry Garnet, p44 KB 27/1522/2 Coram Rege Rolls, initial detail, James I, 1623, p44 SP 14/216/2 Warning letter to Lord Monteagle, p45 SP 14/216 Pt2 (11) (11 of 11) Thomas Wintour's signature on confession, p46 SP 14/216 Pt2 (200) Note from Garnet written with orange juice, p58 SP 14/216/2 Warning letter to Lord Monteagle, p59 SP 14/216 Pt2 (165a) Father Henry Garnet

Picture Acknowledgements

Front cover images: All images Shutterstock aside from the following: British Library/Flickr, National Archives SP14-216 and SP14-216, National Archives SP14-216. Back cover images: All images Shutterstock aside from the following: British Library/Flickr, Wikimedia, National Archives SP14/216, National Archives E 329/475.
Inside images: All images Shutterstock aside from the following: p4 top Getty Images, p5 bottom Getting Images, p7 top left John Foxe/Wikimedia, top right, p8 top Sjwells53/Wikimedia, p8 bottom British Library/Robana/Getty Images, p11 bottom Getty Images, p12 top Getty Images, p13 top Getty Images, p12-13 Wikimedia, p15 top Wikimedia, p16 bottom Getty Images, p17 left Wikimedia, p17 right Getty Images, p18-19 bottom Getty Images, p19 top Wikimedia, p20 top Getty Images, p21 bottom British Library/Flickr, p22 bottom Wikimedia, p23 top Wikimedia, p24 top Getty Images, p25 top Wikimedia, p26 top National Portrait Gallery, p27 top National Portrait Gallery, p28-29 top Getty Images, p29 bottom Getty Images, p31 top left National Portrait Gallery, p31 top right Back Ache/Wikimedia, p31 bottom Wikimedia, p32 top Getty Images, p32-33 British Library/Flickr, p33 top Hulton Archive/Stringer/Getty Images, p34 bottom Getty Images, p35 top right Getty Images, p35 bottom Hulton Archive/Getty Images, p36 bottom Getty Images, p37 bottom right David Bjorgen/Wikimedia, p38 left Wikimedia, p39 top right Wikimedia, p42 bottom British Library/Robana/Getty Images, p43 top Getty Images, p43 bottom British Library/Robana/Getty Images, p45 top right Getty Images, p47 top left Getty Images, p47 top right Getty Images, p47 bottom Getty Images, p48 bottom Getty Images, p49 top Wikimedia, p49 bottom Wikimedia, p51 bottom Getty Images, p52 bottom right Getty Images, p23 inset Dominic Alves/Wikimedia, p55 bottom left Wikimedia, p55 bottom right Nobel Foundation/Wikimedia, p56 top Wikimedia, p57 top Getty Images, p57 bottom Keith Seabridge/Flickr.

INDEX